THE
# PAPERCLIP
# RESISTANCE
PROJECT

*Symbols act as a universal shorthand that transcends language barriers, speeds our comprehension and fosters a shared understanding. They connect us to memories, traditions and our history, strengthening our sense of identity and belonging.*

*The paperclip symbolizes connection: linking one person to another, binding communities together and reminding us that even small acts can hold great meaning.*

*a **personal** journal*

# THE
# PAPERCLIP
# RESISTANCE
## PROJECT

*g.*

The idea that we are bound to one another and unified in our desire for a world of inclusivity, freedom, acceptance and a desire to See Good & Do Good, makes one realize, that innumerable acts of kindness, as small as a paperclip, when multiplied, keeps the community lighthouse burning as a beacon of hope for all mankind.

These pages are for you to record your daily journey, writing down personal acts of kindness, then witnessing the magic that happens.

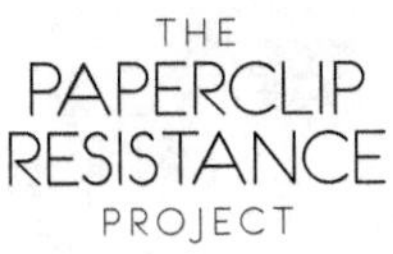

*goodness . . . leading to goodness.*

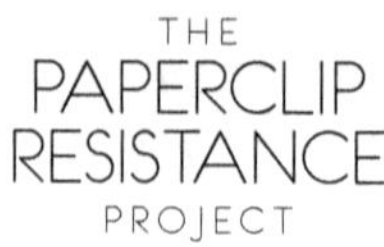



*goodness . . . leading to goodness.*

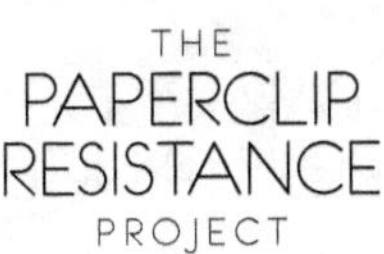

6

*goodness . . . leading to goodness.*

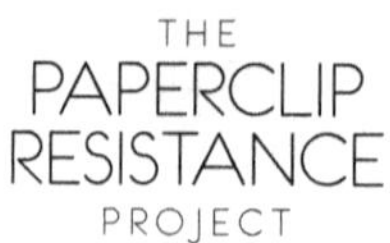



*goodness . . . leading to goodness.*

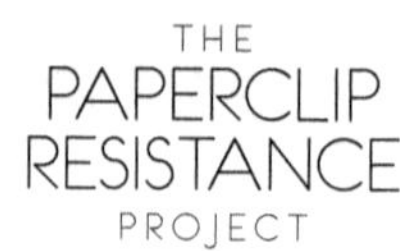





*goodness . . . leading to goodness.*

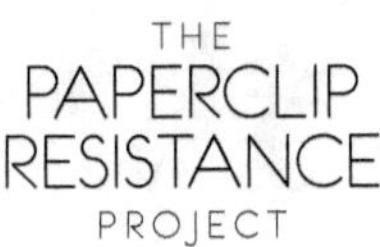



*goodness . . . leading to goodness.*

12

*goodness . . . leading to goodness.*

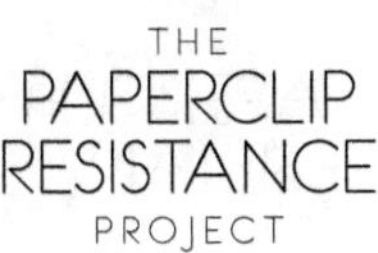



*goodness . . . leading to goodness.*

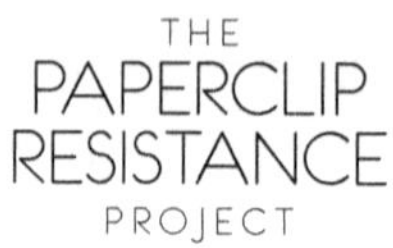





*goodness . . . leading to goodness.*

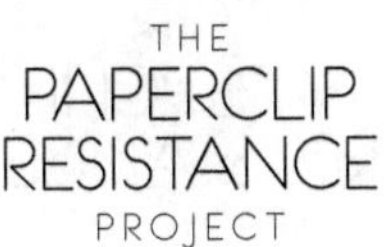

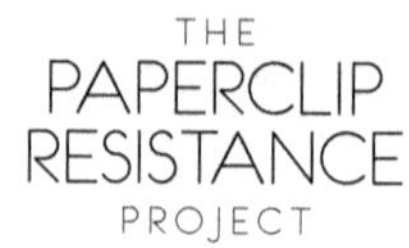



*goodness . . . leading to goodness.*

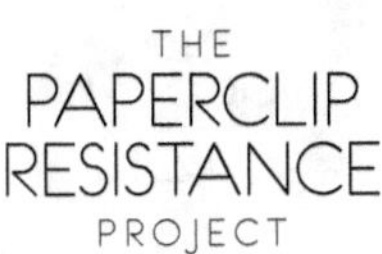

18

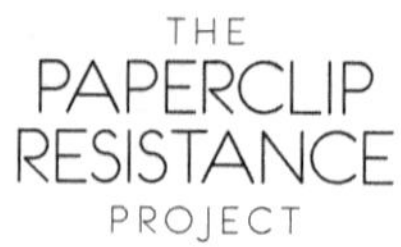



*goodness . . . leading to goodness.*

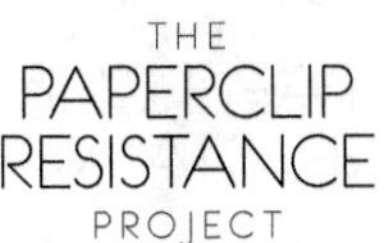

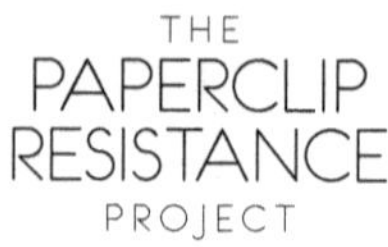



*goodness . . . leading to goodness.*

THE
PAPERCLIP
RESISTANCE
PROJECT

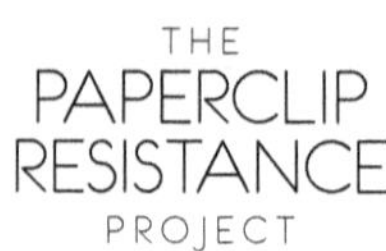



*goodness . . . leading to goodness.*

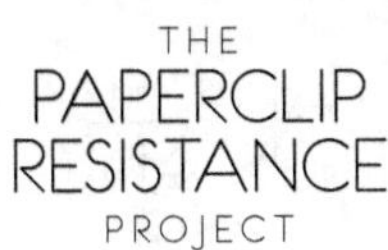



*goodness . . . leading to goodness.*

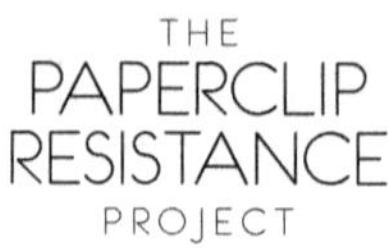



*goodness . . . leading to goodness.*

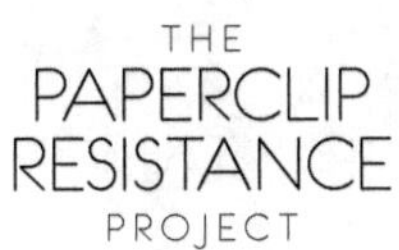

THE
PAPERCLIP
RESISTANCE
PROJECT

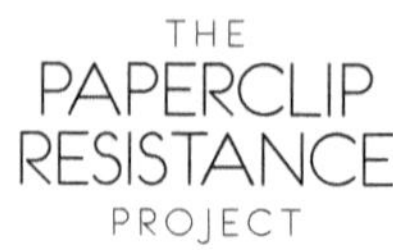



*goodness . . . leading to goodness.*

*goodness . . . leading to goodness.*

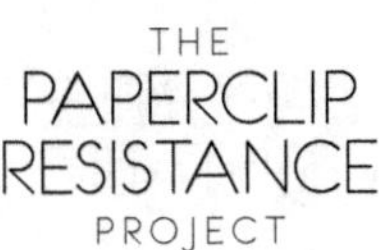

*goodness . . . leading to goodness.*

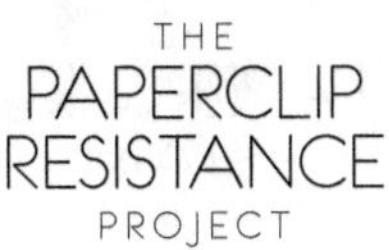

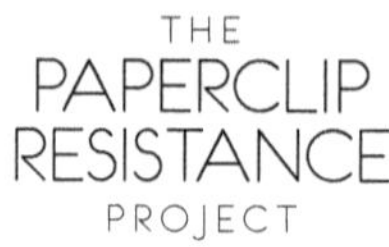





*goodness . . . leading to goodness.*

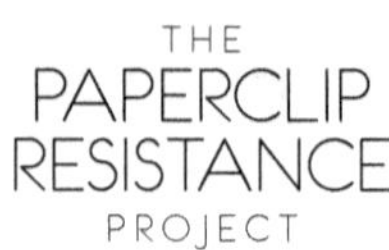



*goodness . . . leading to goodness.*

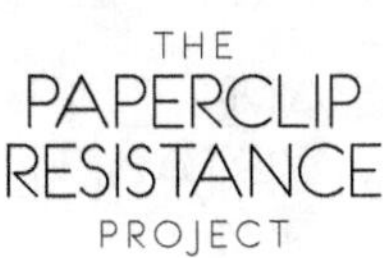



_goodness . . . leading to goodness._

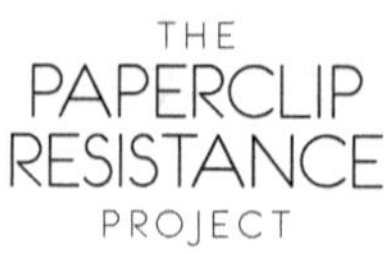




*goodness . . . leading to goodness.*

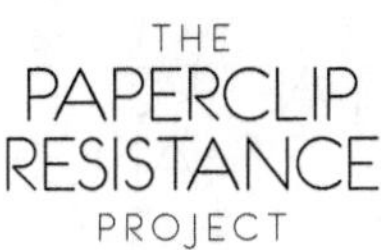

THE
PAPERCLIP
RESISTANCE
PROJECT

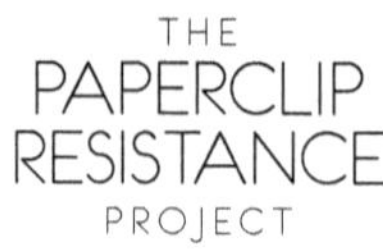





*goodness . . . leading to goodness.*

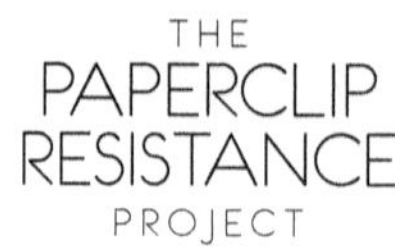



*goodness . . . leading to goodness.*

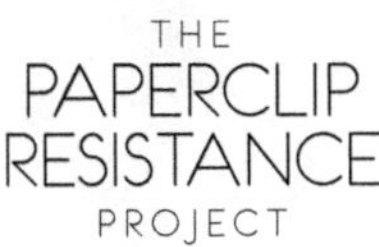

g.



ISBN: 978-1-967254-22-4

**Janice & Ollie Pederson**

206.265.1598 / paperclip.me@outlook.com
thepaperclipresistanceproject.com

*design & production / timmyroland.com*

www.ingramcontent.com/pod-product-compliance
Lightning Source LLC
Chambersburg PA
CBHW051818050726
47598CB00006B/2612